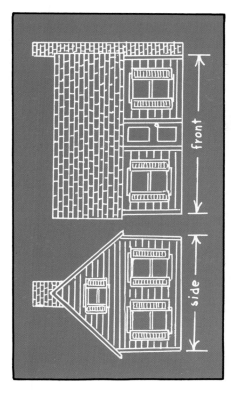

Building a House

by Byron Barton

Greenwillow Books, New York

Building a House. Copyright © 1981 by Byron Barton.
All rights reserved. Manufactured in China by South China
Printing Company Ltd. For information address
HarperCollins Children's Books, a division of
HarperCollins Publishers, 10 East 53rd Street,
New York, NY 10022. www.harperchildrens.com
First Edition 12 13 SCP 10 9
Library of Congress Cataloging-in-Publication Data:
Barton, Byron. Building a house. "Greenwillow Books."
Summary: Briefly describes the steps in building a house.
1. House construction—Juvenile literature.   [1. House
construction.] I. Title. TH4811.5.B37690'.8373 80-22674
ISBN 0-688-80291-5 ISBN 0-688-84291-7 (lib. bdg.)
ISBN 0-688-09356-6 (pbk.)

On a green hill

a machine digs a big hole.

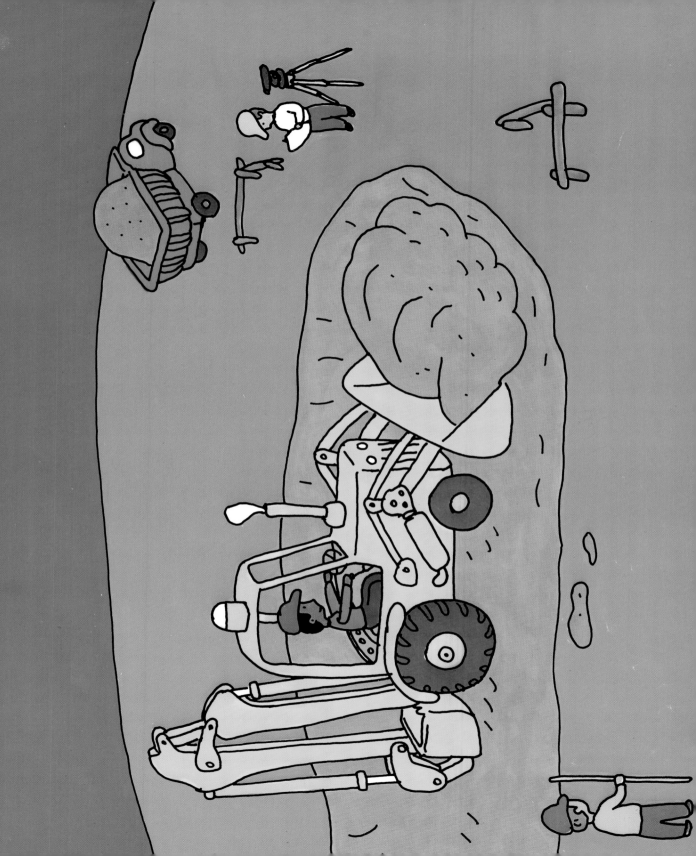

Builders hammer and saw.

A cement mixer pours cement.

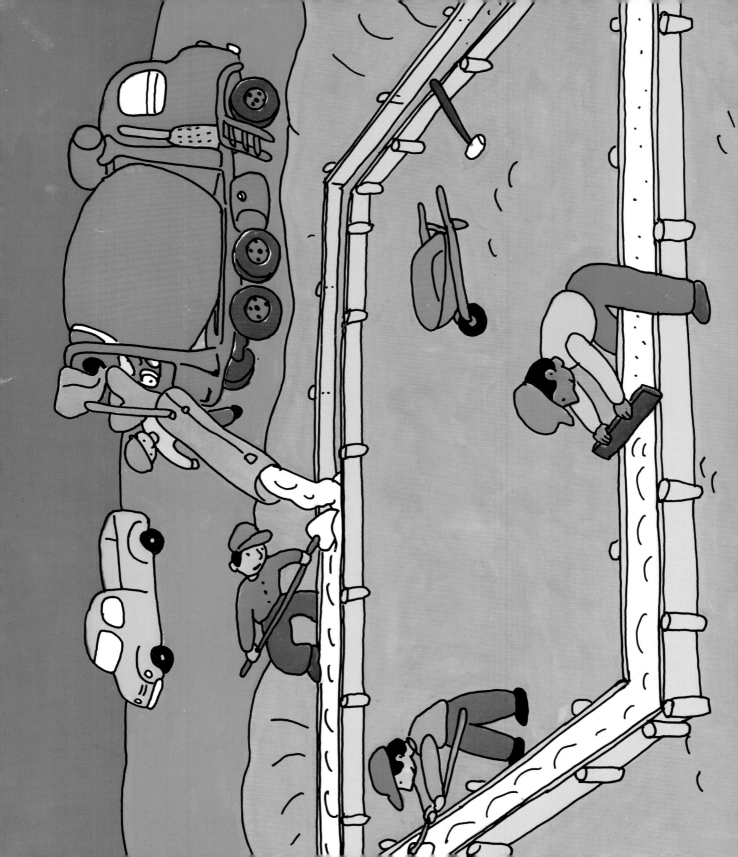

Bricklayers lay large white blocks.

Carpenters come and make a wooden floor.

They put up walls.

They build a roof.

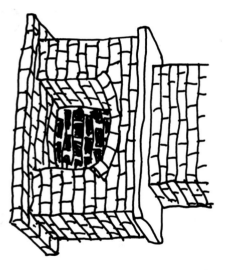

A bricklayer builds a fireplace and a chimney too.

A plumber puts in pipes for water.

An electrician wires for electric lights.

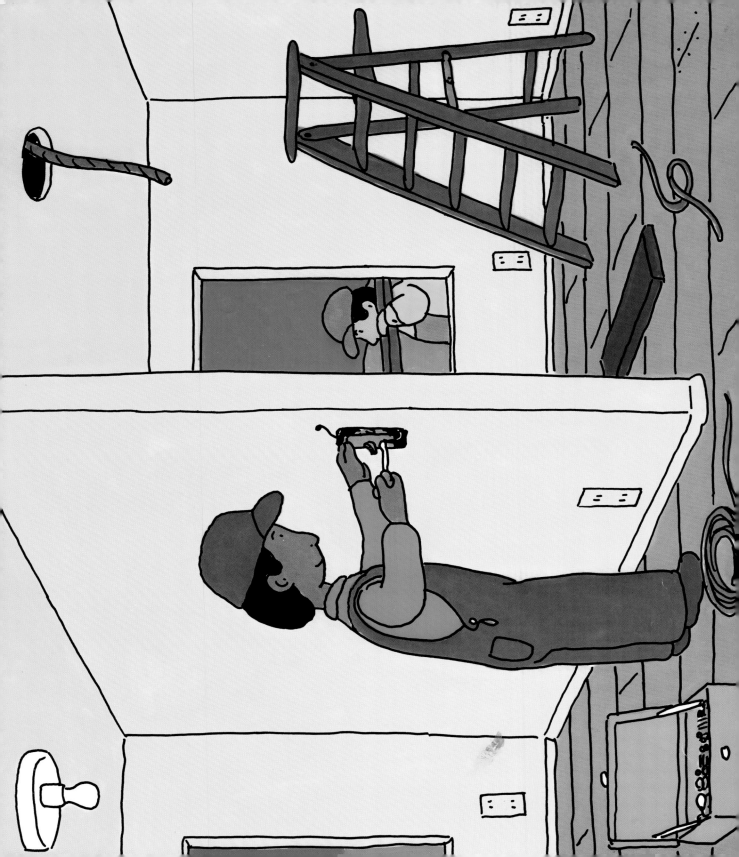

Carpenters put in windows and doors.

Painters paint inside and out.

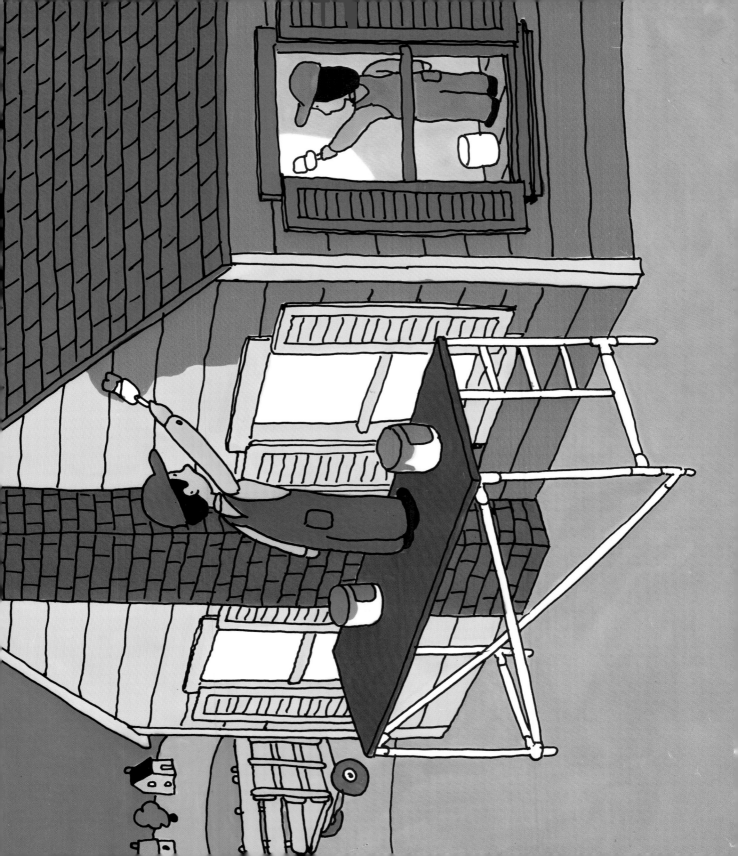

The workers leave.

The house is built.

The family moves inside.